Are You SERIOUS?

Are You SERIOUS?

The epic beginner's guide to becoming an
ACTOR using unorthodox methods.

by

WILL SCOVILLE

Austin, Texas

2019

"It's like the lottery you gotta be in it, to win it!"

~ *Alfred Kenneth Abraham*

TABLE OF CONTENTS

INTRODUCTION

WORK SMARTER

"If you enjoy working smarter to get the best results, congratulations you've come to the right place!"

Before we get this party officially started, I have a quick question for you. Are you serious about becoming an actor? No, I mean, are *you really serious* about becoming an actor? If so, I can help you turn your dreams into a reality!

My name is Will Scoville, I was born and raised in a small town in central New York. I've worked in the entertainment industry since 2006, landing over 45 gigs on my own without the help of a talent agent. Those jobs included student films, independent projects, and large scale productions like *Friday*

Night Lights and Robert Rodriguez's *Machete*. After getting a few bit parts, I scored starring roles in the indie cult sensation *Serial Rabbit 3; Splitting Hares!, The Green Conspiracy, Voice of the Unknown, A Paranormal Investigation,* and *Serial Rabbit V, The Epic Hunt.* In addition to my acting accomplishments, I was honored to serve on the board of the San Antonio Film Council from 2016-2017.

Are You Serious? contains exclusive knowledge that I've obtained while working in the business for over ten years! My book is a comprehensive five-step process created to empower beginning actors to successfully overcome the challenges of finding work in today's entertainment industry.

"A great actor doesn't wait for an opportunity they create it." ~ Will Scoville

STEP 1

SET A GOAL

"Goal - the object of a person's ambition or effort; an aim or desired result."

Now that you've purchased my book, *and I do appreciate that* it's time to ask the obvious question, "What's your goal?"

Be bold, don't hold back, and reach for the stars! In the entertainment industry, there are so many exciting opportunities to choose from. For instance, you can become a sports entertainment performer, an engaging talk show host, a spectacular performance artist, a tv news correspondent, a radio personality, a dynamic social media content creator, or even a brilliant film, television, theater, or web series actor. Choose an option and start your journey!

One step at a time.

It's important to take one step at a time to achieve your goal to avoid being overwhelmed. After completing my five-step process you'll be able to map out a logical career path that will stream-line your road to success.

1. *Identify your objectives and sub-objectives*, i.e. the steps and substeps required to achieve a goal. The information contained in the subsequent chapters will help bring clarity to this process. But for now, here's a sample of a career path outline to give you a visual.

Career Path Sample Outline:

Goal:

Become a Dynamic Social Media Content Creator/Actor.

Objectives and Sub-objectives:

Acquire a Skillset (Learn the fundamentals of your craft.)
- Enroll in online acting lessons.
- Take a stand-up comedy class.

Hone Your Talent (Practice your craft.)
- Enter 48-hour film festivals with friends.
- Act in Student films.
- Create a variety of social media live feeds.
- Perform in stage plays.

Find a Niche (Choose an area of expertise that suits you.)
- Decide to become a hilarious comedy vlogger.

Land That Job (Creatively finding employment.)
- Create a YouTube channel, monetize, sell merch, etc.

2. *Implement your plan* and work hard to accomplish it. Execute all objectives and sub-objectives from top to bottom. If success were effortless then every wannabe thespian would become the next Matthew McConaughey.

3. *Attain your goal* by keeping your eyes on the prize. Always maintain focus in the face of adversity; adapt and overcome!

Even after you've implemented your plan, new opportunities may arise that require your objectives/sub-objectives to evolve. When it comes to planning your future, be flexible and embrace new challenges. This will help you build a resume and grow as an actor.

The Biz: Fantasy vs. Reality.

It's time to pull up your stakes from Fantasy Land and move into your luxury condo on Reality Boulevard. A common fallacy that befalls the uninitiated is the notion that being successful in the industry is as easy as enrolling in acting classes, signing on with a talent agent, and landing a starring role in the next box office hit. The reality is the grind rarely plays out that way. A good example of a plausible scenario is, enroll in acting class, pursue background talent opportunities to get your feet wet and learn set etiquette, shoot a funny YouTube vlog documenting your daily experiences, perform in a live stage play, score a couple of industrial video gigs, move on to bit parts in small budget projects, hire a reputable talent agent, and continue to ascend onward and upward.

Don't let people shite on your dream!

Never be discouraged by naysayers. I've experienced my fair share of glass-half-empty negative Nellies over the years, and have mightily triumphed over their onslaught of sticks and stones. Granted, not all of my past acquaintances were turds, quite the contrary, most of them thought my career was pretty badass! I adore the entertainment industry, having been part of some incredible productions! In the end, the sweet smell of success is the best F-U you could ever deliver to your detractors. If you don't quit, you win!

When a door opens up, run straight through it, don't walk! How I set and attained a goal.

An area of deep-rooted passion for me is the wacky world of professional championship wrestling. I'm a real-life third-generation wrestling fanatic! As a little kid, I can still recall sitting on a big couch adorned by colorful nature patterns next to my grandma and grandpa as they ritualistically spent each Saturday night glued to the television set. Heckling the heels and cheering the babyfaces as the ring generals masterfully worked their craft. Heck, even my dad at the age of 74, is an avid pro wrestling fan who never misses a show!

In the summer of 2006 at the bright young age of 39, I received the opportunity of a lifetime. That year I met my good friend Eddie Guill while working in Austin, TX. This guy was mountain of a man, weighing in at 450 lbs at a height of 6' 5". After a few passing conversations I realized we had something very special in common, we were both wrestling enthusiasts! Eddie revealed that he was not only a fan, but also a pro wrestler on the indy circuit, performing under the ring name, Demonseed. The name was a bit concerning, but he seemed like a nice guy. Come to find out, Eddie is a real-life Texas hardcore wrestling icon!

During one of our lively wrestling conversations, Eddie much to my surprise, gave me an invitation to come to the arena and train! I was flabbergasted, the mere thought set me back on my heels. Initially, I scoffed at the notion, but inwardly I was pumped. After a very brief deliberation I decided to set a goal to *become a live sports entertainment performer!*

My initial objectives were to train to the best of my ability, gain a level of proficiency to adequately work in the ring, perform in front of a live audience, and have a friggin blast! The plan was a bit crude at best, but turned out to be a real winner in the end. Without procrastination, I signed up and started classes right away. After enduring several grueling one hundred degree plus training sessions under a hot tin roof, I was ready to embark on my part-time career as an independent professional wrestler. It was an honor to train under the tutelage of top veteran performers like Russell "Psycho" Simpson and Manny Domingo. Straightaway, I chose the ring name Ironwill Anderson. My family and friends have always referred to me as Bill or Billy, but I picked the name Ironwill, because Ironbill just sounded ridiculous! I hijacked the surname of Anderson from wrestling's infamous tag team The Minnesota Wrecking Crew. The Wrecking Crew members were native Minnesotan's and wrestling legends, Gene and Ole Anderson. Why not pilfer a name from the very best? My only aspiration at the time was

to simply be the best I can be, nothing more, nothing less. Clawing to the next level and receiving some imaginary six-figure contract with a top professional wrestling organization was never in the cards. Due to my age, size, and interest level, becoming the next big wrestling federation champion was simply ludicrous. The mere fact I was able to get in the ring and perform for cheering and sometimes jeering spectators left me stoked! I never thought a childhood dream would ever become a reality. But such as life goes, things happen! Live sports entertainment performer goal, *achieved!*

STEP 2

ACQUIRE A SKILLSET

"In all your getting, get some training!"

Acquiring a sound skillset will exponentially increase your odds of getting meaningful work in the entertainment industry.

Before you start ravaging the internet for the most amazing acting guru ever to grace God's green earth, it may be beneficial to know what type of learner you are. By figuring out this juicy little self-nugget, you can maximize your efforts during training. One popular theory is that there are four different types of learners; visual, auditory, reading/writing and kinesthetic. Visual learners prefer to see information and visualize the relationships between concepts. Auditory learners prefer to listen to information rather than reading or seeing it displayed. Reading/Writing learners prefer interacting with text, they believe it to more powerful for them than hearing or seeing images. Kinesthetic learners are a more hands-on, mastery by doing type of individual. Most people prefer to utilize a combination of these techniques to fully master their craft. Customize your training process with the kind of learning that suits you best.

No ~~pain~~ train, no gain!

There's a lot of viable options for mastering your craft, so let's explore! If formal classroom training is what you crave, then get your fix by surfing the internet to find a local college, university, theater, or performing arts institute.

Another fantastic option is to find a local acting coach and take lessons. A simple online search should produce results for instructors in your area. Once you've compiled a shortlist of coach candidates, look for client reviews, and always check imdb.com to view their acting resume. Every great coach should be able to practice what they preach.

Discovering a viable candidate by joining a social media group that caters to local actors and/or casting agencies is another good option. A simple search, ex. *Austin actors group* will turn up favorable results for the Austin area. Plugin your city and roll the dice!

Never discount the human element in your search. Look for local monthly film industry network mixers. This a great way to hobnob with like-minded people in a relaxed social environment. It's also the perfect opportunity to get introduced to industry professionals and quite possibly to an acting coach. Some coaches offer online training on dedicated websites such as MasterClass.com. Again, check internet reviews and make an informed decision.

No dinero, no problemo.

Don't get derailed by the cost of acting classes or your inability to attend formal training. There's hundreds, if not thousands of online training alternatives to choose from. If cost is the issue, several YouTube content creators provide free acting lessons. Do your due diligence when selecting a coach. Read video comments and watch/evaluate the instruction before making your final decision.

The less obvious, but effective way of gaining some knowledge is to watch and evaluate other actor's performances. Whether it be in the form of a play, film, or television series, observe other actors as they work their craft. If their performances seem wonky and don't appear to be natural or believable, it's not good acting.

A rolling stone gathers no moss.

Don't fall into the analysis paralysis trap. Pondering endless possibilities and never moving forward is the kiss death to any budding acting career. There's no better time for action than the present!

How I acquired my skillset.

My initial training began in the wrestling ring. Taking bumps, learning wrestling moves, and selling my gimmick to crowds of rabid wrestling fans. To be perfectly clear, the crowds numbered less than 250 spectators, but the numbers weren't my motivation. It wasn't about the size of the audience, it was about the fun of performing! In the beginning, ring veterans Russell Simpson and Manny Domingo put me through the paces in a building that was so freaking hot, I exited the arena on my very first day of training after only 25 minutes due to getting "Blowed up" a.k.a., heat exhaustion. Not to be deterred, I dragged my warm carcass back to the arena the very next day, and so on.

Eventually, learning enough to competently grapple in the squared circle.

Hard work pays off!

In late 2006 I was cast in the indy feature film, Fighting With Anger starring Willie Nelson, directed by martial arts Grandmaster, Sam Um. While filming on location I was approached by Sam and he asked if I was interested in training at his martial arts studio. Upon hearing this music to my ears, I sounded off with a resounding, "Heck Yeah!" The thought of learning new skills and translating them to the big screen was very appealing to me. During the seven years of training with Grandmaster Um, I landed one gig right after another, utilizing my ninja-like skillset. Of course, that's being a bit cheeky, but I did rather well and acquired enough talent to become competent in my actions.

A fun fact is that I was one of the original members of Fighting Stunts Association and Action Film Institute founded by Grandmaster Wonik Yi, Sr. Master Ali Brown, and Janell Smith. As a member of FSA, I attended classes featuring various fighting and stunt related techniques, and even received the opportunity to participate in Black Belt Complexes training with Australian Martial Arts Hall of Famer, Richard Norton. It was a complete honor to learn from Richard, who appeared in the 1980 Chuck Norris film, *The Octogaon* and worked on over eighty feature films and television programs.

Keep training don't just bullshit your way through it.

After landing the starring role of Det. Harvey in the Texas indie cult sensation Serial Rabbit III; Splitting Hares in 2009, I decided to look for a local acting coach after struggling with dialogue during production. I was able to "Bullshit" my way through it, but internally I wasn't satisfied with my effort. The inability to properly memorize lines put me at a great disadvantage. During this time, my good friends, Shawne Groves and Allison Gersch were taking lessons from acting coach, Marco Perella. They encouraged me to sign up and attend the training. Learning techniques from the very best certainly has it's advantages. Marco gave me the tools I needed to help increase my chances of success in the entertainment business.

Acting class spoiler alert!

I learned that if I ran my lines fifteen times in a row, not thirteen, not fourteen, but the magical fifteen, I could remember almost any dialogue. Now, I'm able to focus on all the little nuances of a role rather than struggle with lines.

STEP 3

HONE YOUR TALENT

"Practice doesn't make perfect, but you'll be a whole lot better than you were before!"

Now that you've set your goal and acquired a skillset, it's time to transform that lumpy piece of coal into a big-ass diamond!

Like a thoroughbred chomping at the bit, ready to burst threw the gate, I bet you're super jacked to land a starring role in the next *Transformers* movie, right? But before you start perusing the MLS for a Beverly Hills mansion, you'll need to develop your skills. The next logical step in the process is to create some practice opportunities in order to hone your talent.

Gazillions of opportunities!

That's right, there are gazillions (Yeah it's a real word, look it up!) of ways to score some quality practice time, here's a few examples to get the ball rolling.

- Reach out to your local university's RTF department and inquire about students who are searching for talent to act in their projects.

- Enter a local 48-hour film contest with your friends. A cursory internet search may provide upcoming event details and information.

- Contact your local playhouse to ask about upcoming audition opportunities for new plays.

- Utilize a cell phone and your favorite social media platform (Facebook, YouTube, Instagram, etc.) to produce short videos. For example, you can make funny vlogs and talk about interesting topics or even review the latest movie you've watched.

- Contact background talent agencies in your area and apply. Even in a background capacity, you'll gain invaluable experience. Observing how a large scale production operates is a great learning opportunity. Put the cell phone away and take in all the glory that surrounds you.

- Check the local classifieds for acting opportunities. Here's my PSA for ya, ask plenty of questions before showing up for an audition and never meet up alone or in a potentially unsafe environment, especially females. Your safety is always number one!

- Use your cell to produce videos of yourself performing a skit that you wrote or reenact a scene from your favorite movie, then critique the performance. Incorporate others when possible, fun times!

- Attend local film network mixers and find productions you can take part in. Lots of filmmakers, producers, directors, actors, etc. show up at these functions. It's a great opportunity to find potential gigs and get to know others in the entertainment industry.

- Create a blog talk radio show and air a weekly program.

Commit to the process and take your craft seriously. With modern-day mobile technology, there's no excuse not to practice. You can do it, now "Git-R-done!"

My skill honing process began by taking every damn project that was tossed in my general direction, and I loved it! It was great practice and the source of many amazing networking opportunities. Actively searching for and landing roles in student films, commercials, 48-hour film festivals, low budget productions, film teasers, and trailers allowed me to keep refining my skillset while building an acting resume. Lots of wins associated with staying active in the film industry scene, work begets work. Avoid long lapses in-between projects, because, in this biz, it's out of sight out of mind. Words to the wise; *Keep working to stay relevant!*

The only time I was kinda disappointed in a role was when my good friend Edward Burlett and I were asked to help with a 48-hour horror film festival submission by a mutual acquaintance. I remember both of us being super stoked about the whole idea. Who could blame us, we were new to the business and felt it was an opportunity of a lifetime! While on set I overheard a crew member say that our scene centered around an old couch. The director had the crew modify the sofa by cutting out small hand-sized holes that ran from the back to front. Curious, and still a bit delusional regarding the importance of our roles, we anxiously anticipated our big scene.

The hands from hell, a horror story.

As time passed, reality began to set in as the director explained that we would be positioning ourselves behind the couch, and on action, reach through and attempt to grab the principal actors. No face-time, no lines, nothing but the hands from hell! In essence, we were glorified hand models. Not quite the outcome we had hoped for, but at the end of the day, we were able to partake in a good laugh. Lessons-learned; regardless of your part, be the consummate professional, and never leave home without clipping your fingernails!

STEP 4

FIND YOUR NICHE

"Choose a job you love, and you will never have to work a day in your life."

Seek and you shall find! Whether choreographing dynamic fight scenes, vlogging, theater acting, miming, fire juggling, print work, making industrial videos, film acting, or radio broadcasting, you should have little difficulty finding a job you thoroughly enjoy. Most people don't realize all the potential opportunities that exist for today's actor. With all the available platforms, the only out of work actor is the one who lacks knowledge, creativity, and motivation. Now that you have all of the above, it's time to make a decision.

Oh, the decisions!

I've compiled a list of areas you may like to specialize in. My recommendation would be to choose the one that resonates with you, sit down, write out your career path as outlined in Step 1, and get to work.

<u>Film</u>

- Actor.
- Voice over actor.
- Background artist.
- Utility stand-in.
- Photo double.
- Body double.
- Hand double.
- Minor double.

  * Create a film and upload it to Amazon.

<u>Television</u>

- Actor.
- Voice over actor.
- Background artist.
- Multi-camera stand-in.
- Single-camera stand-in.

- Utility stand-in
- Photo double.
- Body double.
- Hand double.
- Minor double.

* Create a series and upload it to Amazon.

Radio

- On-air personality.
- Reporter/interviewer.
- Blog talk show creator.
- Podcaster.

Social Media

Create content based on your interests and knowledge. Produce quality pieces using the best equipment you can afford. Monetize your content according to platform guidelines.

- YouTube content creator.
- Facebook live streaming.
- Instagram live streaming.
- Twitch gamer.
- Patreon content creator.
- Podcast creator.

Performance Art

- Music.
- Opera.
- Theater.
- Magic.
- Illusion.
- Spoken word.
- Puppetry.
- Circus.
- Sports entertainment.

Don't be a rabbit.

I want to stress the importance of mastering a given area. Don't hop around from niche to niche, until you've mastered at least one. Being known as an expert in any given area will bolster your brand, being the master of none, will not.

STEP 5

LAND THAT JOB

"The best way to star in a film is to make your own."
~ Brett Mauser, Filmmaker

You've been grinding away, working long hard hours, honing your skills, and now you're ready to land your dream job! Not so fast, if it were that simple everyone would do it. But since you were diligent and kept your eyes on the prize, the odds have exponentially increased in your favor.

A conventional mindset is a losing mindset.

Many new actors are very conventional in thought and deed. For instance, the old way of making a career in the entertainment business was pretty straight forward. Attend acting classes, find a talent agent, chase auditions, land a job or two, and eventually lose interest and fade into the sunset. Don't get me wrong, there are amazing success stories, but some people win the lottery, too! The seemingly long list of successful working actors appears rather impressive until you factor in all the unemployed actors. According to a June 5, 2019 article found in The Guardian, only 2% of actors make a living from the profession and 90% are out of work at any one time.

Don't despair, amazing gigs come in many forms!

Now it's time to break away from the stereotypical idea of what an acting opportunity looks like. Let's explore the possibilities.

- If you insist on pursuing the conventional route, you may search the interweb for a talent agent to chase that ever-elusive tv/film/theatrical audition or print work. With your previous training and practice, there's a decent chance you can score a reputable agent right out of the gate. Perform your due diligence and make a wise selection. You'll want to have a current professional headshot and an acting resume. Ensure that both are up to industry standard.

- If you haven't done so already, apply with a local casting agency specializing in background talent. Not only can you get hooked up with a background gig but sometimes when you're on set, if you possess the right look, skillset, and the storyline calls for it, you may even land a featured extra role or even rock a couple lines of dialogue. The bump in pay is pretty sweet!

- Create a YouTube channel and start a daily show. With so many topics to choose from, pick one that interests you and will appeal to an audience. While most would-be actors focus on the norm (Film and television gigs.), the smart choice is alternative platforms. This puts the control squarely in your hands. The creation, production, and promotion are all your babies now! The reach is far greater than most television networks, YouTube is worldwide! Like all endeavors, success doesn't come without its share of innovative ideas and sweat equity. Produce the best quality show within your budget and strive for excellence. With modern-day mobile technology, you can accomplish your mission on a modest budget.

- Another sweet option to get your acting fix is to create a Patreon account. Again you'll need the same equipment and of course a great show or video series idea. With Patreon you can offer various monthly levels of support for your patrons.

- If you're a gamer, a site like Twitch may provide that spare change you're looking for. Utilize your acting skills while playing your favorite video games. Earn money through the addition of subscribers, Twitch affiliate and partner programs, ad revenue, donations, paid live streams, sponsorships, and more.

- Produce a quality film or series and upload it to Amazon. As quoted previously, *"The best way to star in a film is to make your own."* The more hats you can wear in the process the lower your costs will be. Organize your team, film, edit, subtitle, upload, and promote. This is an oversimplification of the production processes, but if you can accomplish everything you need to get done, then you're well on your way to receiving that lovely Amazon monthly royalty deposit. You can watch plenty of videos online for advice on every step of the process.

- Scour your local classifieds to see what paying gigs are available. As mentioned previously, be safe when meeting up with potential employers.

- Not to sound redundant, but attending network mixers that's inundated with industry professionals is a great way to meet casting directors, talent agents, producers, and other poeple who may help in furthering your acting career.

With all the aforementioned suggestions and any creative ideas you may have, there's no reason you should be an unemployment statistic. Believe in the process; believe in yourself!

When word of mouth was king!

I found success using a combination of some of the previously noted methods to gain meaningful employment. Initially, word of mouth was king. Showing up to set on time, having a great attitude, and doing a good job will open up many doors. Cultivating relations with other cast and crew members was beneficial as well. It's much more enjoyable working 12-15 hours a day with people you like and admire than it is hanging out with a bag of assholes. With that being said, be good to everyone and keep a positive attitude on the job, you never know where that next job referral will come from.

Landing some extra/stand-in work after signing on with a talent agency proved to be a good source of additional income and a valuable learning experience for me. I found that networking with fellow actors during downtime, observing cast and crew interactions, and seeing how each person worked their craft was time well spent. Another important aspect of being on set was learning how to take direction. Valuable time is wasted if a director or other crew member have to repeat instructions, time is money. Remember to always keep your head in the game while you're on the clock. Stay professional and stand out for all the right reasons.

My big break!

After performing fight scenes and stuntwork on a handful of Innocence Saga films for director, Brett Mauser, I finally received my big break. Brett ask if I was interested in the role of Detective Harvey in the now indie cult sensation, *Serial Rabbit III; Splitting Hairs*. I felt overwhelmed by my emotions, all the training, all the bit parts, all the work had lead me to this day, a starring role in a feature film! From there I ended up starring in a few more features for Brett and I can honestly say, I am forever in his debt for believing in me and providing some of the most amazing times in my acting career. He always fed us, treated everyone with great respect, gave new actors a platform to work their craft, premiered the films at outstanding venues, helped validate our brands by adding each project to IMDb, and provided a family-like atmosphere during filming.

Do it yourself!

After working on several productions of all shapes and sizes I decided to create my very own film magic. With the help of Edward Burlett, we were able to produce multiple projects. The most notable, *Voice of the Unknown, A Paranormal Investigation.* I can't stress enough the importance of being attentive to everything that happens on set. It can pay off dividends in the future, if and when you decide to venture out on your own. The more you can do yourself, i.e. film, sound, lighting, direct, act, video/sound editing, promotional graphics, etc. the easier it will be to bang out projects.

Make YouTube your friend, a lot of available instruction is on there for those who look for it. If you have to pay other people to do every little fooken thing associated with your production, then you're not going to accomplish much unless of course you hit all five numbers and the Powerball!

Once you've created your cinematic masterpiece, Amazon is an outstanding platform to upload the finished work. You also need to know that when you upload a video, you must include a separate subtitle file. It's relatively inexpensive to pay for a service to subtitle your work. Once your film is live, it's up to you to promote your project and get those clicks. Amazon will pay a monthly royalty based upon minutes watched for Prime subscribers. You'll also receive a cut of any video rental and/or purchases.

Keep your eyes on the prize!

No process can guarantee a 100% success rate, but without a sound game plan, the odds of achieving your goals are slim to none. Follow my five-step process and keep your eyes on the prize and you'll increase your chances of success exponentially.

In conclusion.

My first love was on-screen fighting and stuntwork. With a wrestling background and ongoing martial arts training, I felt like I was adequately equipped to professionally work my niche. After additional training and acting classes, I felt confident enough to pursue speaking roles in which I landed my fair share. Remember, the work is there for those who prepare!

Gratitude.

If you're a new actor, I truly believe that with my five-step process you can put words into action and realize your dreams. Be sure to look me up on social media, I'd love to hear your story and answer any question you may have.
I appreciate you and want to take this time to thank you for reading my book.

Warmest regards!
~ Will

SPECIAL THANKS

TO THE PEOPLE THAT INSPIRED ME AND POSITIVELY IMPACTED MY ACTING CAREER

"Surround yourself with those who fan your flames."

Brittany Scoville	Raven Scoville	Sam Murphy
Pierce Scoville	Ryan Scoville	Brett Mauser
Elizabeth Scoville	Edward Burlett	Jake Jecmenek
Grandmaster Sam Um	George de la Isla	Kazumasa Yokoyama

Russell Simpson	Manny Domingo	Tonya McMeans
Bobby Hall	Eddie Guill	Philip Huddleston
Patty Allieri	Dave Spitz	Brenna Roberts
Ian Faust	Richard Norton	Sr. Master Ali Brown
Willie Nelson	Jon Boatwright	Grandmaster Wonik Yi
Pablo Flores	Jannell Smith	Jody Ross Nolan
Robbie Prince	Seth Lee	Maurice Ripke
Kendall Harker	Mary Hisbrook	Jeff Fahey
Robert Rodriquez	David Von Roehm	Marco Perella
Jade Esteban Estrada	Bradley Bates	Craig Rainey
Elsiemarie Tucci	William Scoville Sr.	Yeshua Hamashiach
Debbie Scoville	David Cathey	Matthew McConaughey
Christian Cisneros	David Jordan	Ben Foster
Jay Pennington	Johanna Goldsmith	Alison Gersch
Shawne Groves	Alyssa Onyx	Robert Stewart
Kyle Chandler	DeMarcus Young	James A. House
Waylon Payne	Dan Clark	Kim Kerley
Mike Roberts	Ernest Martinez	Dana Hee
Sergio Cantu	Robert Guill	Rodrigo Botti
Bill Taylor	Stephen Wagers	Adam Janes
Bling Johnson	Marc Daratt	Trant Batey

Names not in any particular order...

CREDITS AND TRAINING

Film and Video

Seeing Sammy (In-Production) (2019)

Wicked (In-Production) (2019)

Serial Rabbit V, The Epic Hunt (2017)

Second to Last Worst Day of My Life (2015)

Voice of the Unknown, A Paranormal Invest. (2011)

Book of Babylon (2011)

Serial Rabbit 5 (Teaser) (2010)

Machete (2010)

Jeffrey Anderson Zombie Hunter (2010)

Bass Reeves (2010

After the Day 2; Before the Knight (2009)

Easy Way to Die (2009)

Nothing Lasts Forever (2009)

Never Say Goodbye (2009)

Green (2009)

Serial Rabbit 3 (2009)

Shorts (2009)

The Overbrook Brothers (2009)

Potatoehead (2008)

Film and Video cont'd...

Kazam II (2008)

Exhibit H (Bloodshots) (2008)

Lo Que Daria Por Volver (Student film) (2008)

Do You Know Stanley Wright? (Student film) (2008)

Shadow Rises (2008)

Lone Wolf McQuade (Kindly Rewind Comp.) (2008)

Hell Honey (Grindhouse 101 trailer) (2007)

TANK (Grindhouse 101 trailer) (2007)

Big Deke VI (Grindhouse 101 trailer) (2007)

Breath (Student film/short) (2007)

The Dead (Student film/short) (2007)

The Undead (Trailer) (2007)

The Ballerina (2007)

El Mariachi 4 (Unnecessary sequel comp.) (2007)

Back to the Corner (Short) (2007)

Extreme Romance (48 hour film project) (2007)

Open House (Bloodshots) (2007)

Fighting With Anger (2007)

Television

Great Day San Antonio, KENS5 (2015)

Friday Night Lights 2:09 (2007)

Friday Night Lights 1:20 (2007)

Friday Night Lights 1:16 (2007)

Fitness Wise (2007)

Fit for Friday (2007)

Commercials

Verizon Wireless (2008)

Bank of America (2008)

Visa Commercial (2008)

Music Video

Phantoms and Shadows (by MOAM) (2013)

Necesito Salvacion (by Boca Abajo) (2007

Sports Entertainment

Indy Professional Wrestling (QFC/ICPW) (2006-Present)

Print

Karate-Do Magazine vol. 10 (2008)

Training

• Film Acting, Alleywood Studios, Austin, TX, Marco Perella.

• Primadonna Productions, San Antonio, TX, Reel Deal - On Camera, Jade Esteban Estrada. Audition process, slating, monologue, cold reads, and acting techniques.

• Fighting Stunts Association and Action Film Institute, Austin, TX, Grandmaster Wonik Yi. Stunt fighting, action choreography, and acting.

• Fighting Stunts Association and Action Film Institute, Austin, TX, Stunt Workshop, Grandmaster Wonik Yi. Basic break falls (low and medium height) and techniques that apply to high falls. Basic strikes, punches, and kicks. Safety and "selling the technique". Making it look as "real" as possible with precision and timing.

• Fighting Stunts Association and Action Film Institute, Austin, TX, Weapons Training, Grandmaster Wonik Yi. Featured weapon - nunchucks.

Training cont'd...

- Fighting Stunts Association and Action Film Institute, Austin, TX, Richard Norton. Stunt fighting seminar.

- 4th Degree Martial Arts, Austin, TX, Black Belt Complexes, Richard Norton (Australian Martial Arts Hall of Fame). Advanced training drills for developing explosive speed and power.

- Quest for Champions of America, Austin, TX, Professional Wrestling School, Russell Simpson and Manny Domingo. Professional wrestling techniques and ring presence.

- Master Marital Arts, Austin, TX, Taekwondo, Hapkido, Grappling, Grandmaster Sam Um.

- Dojo Kyle, Kyle, TX, Brazilian Jiu-Jitsu and Judo.

- United States Army, basic combat skills.

Voice of the Unknown, A Paranormal Investigation (2011).

ABOUT THE AUTHOR

Will is the proud father of four amazing children, Brittany, Raven, Pierce, and Ryan. He has enjoyed an eclectic lifestyle ranging from teenage amateur bodybuilder, U.S. Army veteran, inventor, marathon runner, indy professional wrestler, stunt performer, actor, director, filmmaker, and author. His capacity to overcome obstacles inspired him to put "Fingers to keyboard" and write, *Are You Serious?*, *The epic beginner's guide to becoming an ACTOR using unorthodox methods* to help beginning actors realize their dreams.

One of the highlights of his career was to fight, get his arm snapped like a twig, and tossed over a bar by country music living legend Willie Nelson for the film, *Fighting With Anger*. Will later landed over 45 gigs on his own. Those jobs included student films, independent projects, and large scale productions like *Friday Night Lights* and Robert Rodriguez's *Machete,* starring Jessica Alba and Jeff Fahey. After getting a few bit parts, Will scored starring roles in the indie cult sensation *Serial Rabbit 3; Splitting Hares!, The Green Conspiracy, Voice of the Unknown, A Paranormal Investigation,* and *Serial Rabbit V, The Epic Hunt.*

In addition to his acting accomplishments, Will was honored to serve on the board of the San Antonio Film Council from 2016-2017.

CPSIA information can be obtained
at www.ICGtesting.com
Printed in the USA
LVHW071424181119
637665LV00005B/1377/P